Parent's Introduction

Whether your child is a beginning reader, a reluctant reader, or an eager reader, this book offers a fun and easy way to encourage and help your child in reading.

Developed with reading education specialists, We Both Read books invite you and your child to take turns reading aloud. On your turn, you read a left-hand page; then your child reads the right-hand page, which is written at a specific reading level. The result is a wonderful reading experience with less frustration and faster reading development!

You may find it helpful to read the entire book aloud yourself the first time, then invite your child to participate the second time. As you read, try to make the story come alive by reading with expression. This will help to model good fluency. It will also be helpful to stop at various points to discuss what you are reading. This will help increase your child's understanding of what is being read.

In some books, a few challenging words are introduced in the parent's text, distinguished with **bold** lettering. Pointing out and discussing these words can help to build your child's reading vocabulary. If your child is a beginning reader, it may be helpful to run a finger under the text as each of you reads. Please also notice that a "talking parent" ⊙ icon precedes the parent's text, and a "talking child" ⊙ icon precedes the child's text.

If your child struggles with a word, you can encourage "sounding it out," but keep in mind that not all words can be sounded out. Your child might pick up clues about a word from the picture, other words in the sentence, or any rhyming patterns. If your child struggles with a word for more than five seconds, it is usually best to simply say the word.

Most of all, remember to praise your child's efforts and keep the reading fun. After you have finished the book, ask a few questions and discuss what you have read together. Rereading this book multiple times may also be helpful for your child.

Try to keep the tips above in mind as you read together, but don't worry about doing everything right. Simply sharing the enjoyment of reading together will increase your child's reading skills and help to start your child off on a lifetime of reading enjoyment!

Ben and Becky on an African Safari

A We Both Read® Book
Level 2
Guided Reading: Level L

———————————————————————————

Text Copyright © 2020 by Sindy McKay
Illustrations Copyright © 2020 by Meredith Johnson

Use of photographs provided by iStock, Shutterstock, and Dreamstime.

We Both Read® is a trademark of Treasure Bay, Inc.

Published by
Treasure Bay, Inc.
PO Box 519
Roseville, CA 95661 USA

Printed in China

Library of Congress Catalog Card Number: 2019911437

ISBN: 978-1-60115-364-7

We Both Read® Books

Visit us online at:
TreasureBayBooks.com

PR-10-21

Ben and Becky
on an African Safari

By Sindy McKay

with illustrations by Meredith Johnson

TREASURE BAY

Last year, my grandparents took my sister Becky and me on a real-life African **safari** in a country called Tanzania. I knew it was going to be superawesome when I looked out the airplane window and saw Mount Kilimanjaro—the highest mountain in Africa!

"I'm going to do so much stuff on this **safari**," I told my sister. "Feed a croc, save an elephant, and roar with the lions!"

Becky rolled her eyes. "Sure you are, Ben. In your dreams!"

Our tour guide, **Akida**, was waiting for us at the airport. He was holding a sign with my grandparents' name on it. Next to **Akida** was his son Kami. He was also holding a sign. It made me laugh! Becky just rolled her eyes again.

We all jumped into a jeep and headed for our camp. On the way, we saw a big, green van coming at us fast in the middle of the road. **Akida** had to drive off the road so it wouldn't hit us!

It was getting dark when we arrived at our camp in the Serengeti National Park. The tents were big and looked like fancy hotel rooms inside!

We ate dinner around a campfire and talked about the animals we hoped to see on the safari. Grandma hoped we'd see some big cats, but I was here to see *all* of the "Big Five": Cape buffalo, leopards, lions, rhinos, and elephants.

At last it was time for bed. Becky stayed in one tent with Grandma and Grandpa. I stayed in another tent with Kami. All night I dreamed about the cool animals I was going to see.

In the morning we loaded up the jeep and set out. Grandpa said he was going to shoot every animal he saw. "With my camera, of course," he added with a wink.

As we drove off, Grandma spotted a cheetah in the distance. "Oh, isn't it beautiful?!"

Becky nodded. "They're the fastest land animals in the world, Grandma!"

Grandpa yelled "Woo-hoo!" as he lifted his camera for a picture. Akida asked Grandpa to please not yell. It can scare the animals away.

Down the road we came upon a troop of baboons. Two of them climbed into our jeep to try to steal our lunches. Becky said baboons are "opportunistic eaters." They will eat anything that is easy to get.

Luckily Akida had packed some extra items. He threw them out the window, and the baboons rushed out to grab them.

Next, we saw some warthogs. Parked behind them was the big green van that had run us off the road the day before. "Maybe the warthogs ran *them* off the road today!" Grandpa joked.

"I wonder what those men are doing out there," Becky said.

"They seem to be just looking at the animals," answered Grandpa.

We soon came upon a herd of Cape buffalo. "That's one of the Big Five," I proudly noted.

"Cape buffalo can remember anyone who has tried to hurt them and will attack if they see them again," Akida told us.

"Who would hurt them?" I asked.

"Poachers," answered Becky and Kami in unison.

Then Grandma pointed excitedly, "I think I see a **leopard**!"

Kami said we were lucky to spot a **leopard**. Leopards hunt at night. They often spend their days hidden in trees or caves. Becky added, "They often eat up in a tree so that other animals can't steal their meal."

Now I had seen two of the Big Five—Cape buffalo and a leopard. Only three to go—a lion, a **rhino**, and an elephant.

We had driven another mile or so when Kami quietly pointed out, "There are your lions, Ben." We were in awe. Grandma said they were so majestically beautiful that she almost cried!

Becky pointed out the other side of the jeep and whispered, "Look there, Ben. **Rhinos**."

"WOO-HOO," I yelled.

"Ben! You can't yell around rhinos!" whispered Kami.

"Why not?" I asked.

I soon got my answer.

One of the huge rhinos started charging toward us! Akida turned the jeep around and punched the accelerator! A rhino can run up to 40 miles per hour and is strong enough to push over a car!

Lucky for us, the rhino quickly gave up and we were safe. Phew!

   Then it was time for lunch. Akida was taking us to a cool place for a picnic. Along the way we saw some zebras. "No two zebras have the same set of stripes," Becky told us.

   Kami grinned. "Your sister knows a lot about animals, Ben!"

As we ate, a tower of giraffes sauntered past. Kami said there used to be a lot more, but many had been killed by **poachers**.

"Over forty percent of the giraffe population has been lost in the last fifteen years," Becky informed us.

"I thought hunting in the park was illegal," Grandpa exclaimed.

Akida shrugged, "Some people do it anyway. They don't care about the animals. They only care about making money."

Grandpa was very upset by this. "Those **poachers** better hope I never catch them."

After lunch, we headed out again. We hadn't gone far when we began to smell something awful! Kami laughed. "That's the hippo pool. This pool can have over one hundred hippos in it at once!"

Grandma plugged her nose. "I bet that smell keeps the poachers away!"

I didn't care about the smell. I wanted to go look at a hippo up close! Kami didn't think that was safe. "A hippo can kill you." Then he pointed to another animal in the pool. "If a crocodile doesn't eat you first."

I stayed right where I was.

21

We saw lots more animals that afternoon, but no elephants.

Then, just as we were headed back to camp, we spotted a herd! Akida pointed out a lion that was trying to snatch one of the baby elephants. The whole herd stepped in to **protect** the baby and chase the lion away.

Akida told us it's rare for a lion to take down an elephant. "Elephant moms **protect** every baby in the herd. But sadly, they can't protect them from everything."

"You mean humans," said Grandpa.

Akida nodded. "After dinner I will show you what I mean."

That evening, Akida unlocked the tall gates of the animal **sanctuary** behind our cabins. Before we entered, Becky noticed the big green van we had been seeing was parked under some trees in the distance. She started to ask Kami what the van was doing there but was interrupted by the sound of Grandma squealing happily.

Inside the animal **sanctuary** Grandma had found two young lion cubs. They were so cute! But sadly their mother had been trapped and taken by poachers.

Then Grandpa called us over to look at a baby elephant. "This little guy sure does know how to have fun," he said with a smile.

Kami told us they had found him standing by his mother's body. Poachers had killed her for her tusks. In fact, most of the animals at the sanctuary had been orphaned or hurt by poachers.

That made Grandpa very, very angry. Kami said the poachers must have been scared away or they would have taken the baby to sell to a zoo or some other place.

Becky was full of facts, as usual. "Elephants use their tusks to dig, lift things, gather food, strip bark to eat, and as weapons to defend themselves. They're made of ivory, and some humans will pay a lot of money for ivory."

The baby elephant was very gentle. He let me touch his trunk. It felt like wrinkled leather.

On the way out, we passed a crocodile. Kami said it had been hit by a car and its jaw was hurt. He threw the croc some meat from a freezer box.

"It has a hard time eating," he said. "It can still swallow, but it can't really bite."

That night at camp we heard a pack of noisy hyenas making all kinds of sounds—grunts, whoops, howls, and something that sounded like human laughter!

Then we heard another sound, coming from the sanctuary. The little elephant was crying. "Maybe he's in **trouble**," said Grandpa. "I'll go check on him! I know where the key is!"

Grandma stopped Grandpa. She told him that he would be in big **trouble** if he went to the sanctuary without Akida! Akida came over and told Grandpa not to worry. The animals were safe inside the sanctuary. Finally, we all went to bed, tired from our busy day.

I was dreaming of riding a rhinoceros across the savannah when I felt someone shaking my shoulder. I opened my eyes to see Becky standing over me. "Grandpa is gone," she quietly hissed.

My eyes popped open. I knew right away what Grandpa had done.

Kami woke up and I told him, "Grandpa went to check on the little elephant. We have to bring him back before Grandma finds out!"

Kami grabbed a lantern and we hurried to the sanctuary. We found the gate swinging open. "Someone cut the lock," I gasped as I pointed to the severed lock dangling from the latch.

Becky spotted the big green van parked nearby. "Something weird is going on."

We began to look for Grandpa. "I've got a bad feeling about this," I said. "The animals are all awake. They seem upset!"

"Animals can tell when something is wrong," whispered Becky. "We should be very careful!"

We found Grandpa on the ground next to the baby elephant. But something wasn't right. Grandpa was looking at something that we couldn't see. He looked angry and scared. I started to call to him, but Becky stopped me. We quietly peeked around the corner to see . . .

... POACHERS! WITH GUNS!!

Thinking fast, I came up with a plan. I whispered to Becky, "Open the crocodile pen." Becky smiled. She knew what I was thinking. Then I took a hunk of meat from the freezer box and threw it at the poachers' feet.

The crocodile burst from his open pen and galloped toward the meat! The poachers screamed like hyenas! They didn't know that the croc couldn't really bite.

One of them accidentally shot his gun into the air, alerting the camp. Within moments, Akida and several other guides arrived and arrested the poachers while the crocodile happily gulped down his snack.

Grandpa was so proud of us! We had saved the day!

Becky grinned at me. "So that's *two* things you can check off your list, Ben. You fed a crocodile and you saved an elephant. All that's left now is to roar with the lions!"

The rest of our trip was not quite as exciting as that night, but it was still pretty amazing. Becky and I were both sad when it came time to say goodbye. Kami and I promised to write, and Akida promised to keep Grandpa updated on the progress of the baby elephant.

As we drove off down the road to the airport, we heard a lion roar. Becky, Kami, and I roared back! Then we laughed together one last time.

Now I had done it all.

If you liked *Ben and Becky on an African Safari,* here are some other We Both Read books you are sure to enjoy!

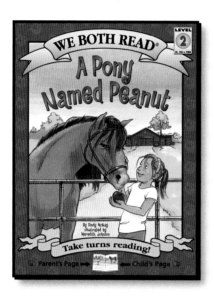

To see all the We Both Read books that are available,
just go online to **WeBothRead.com**.